This Book Belongs To

COLOR TEST

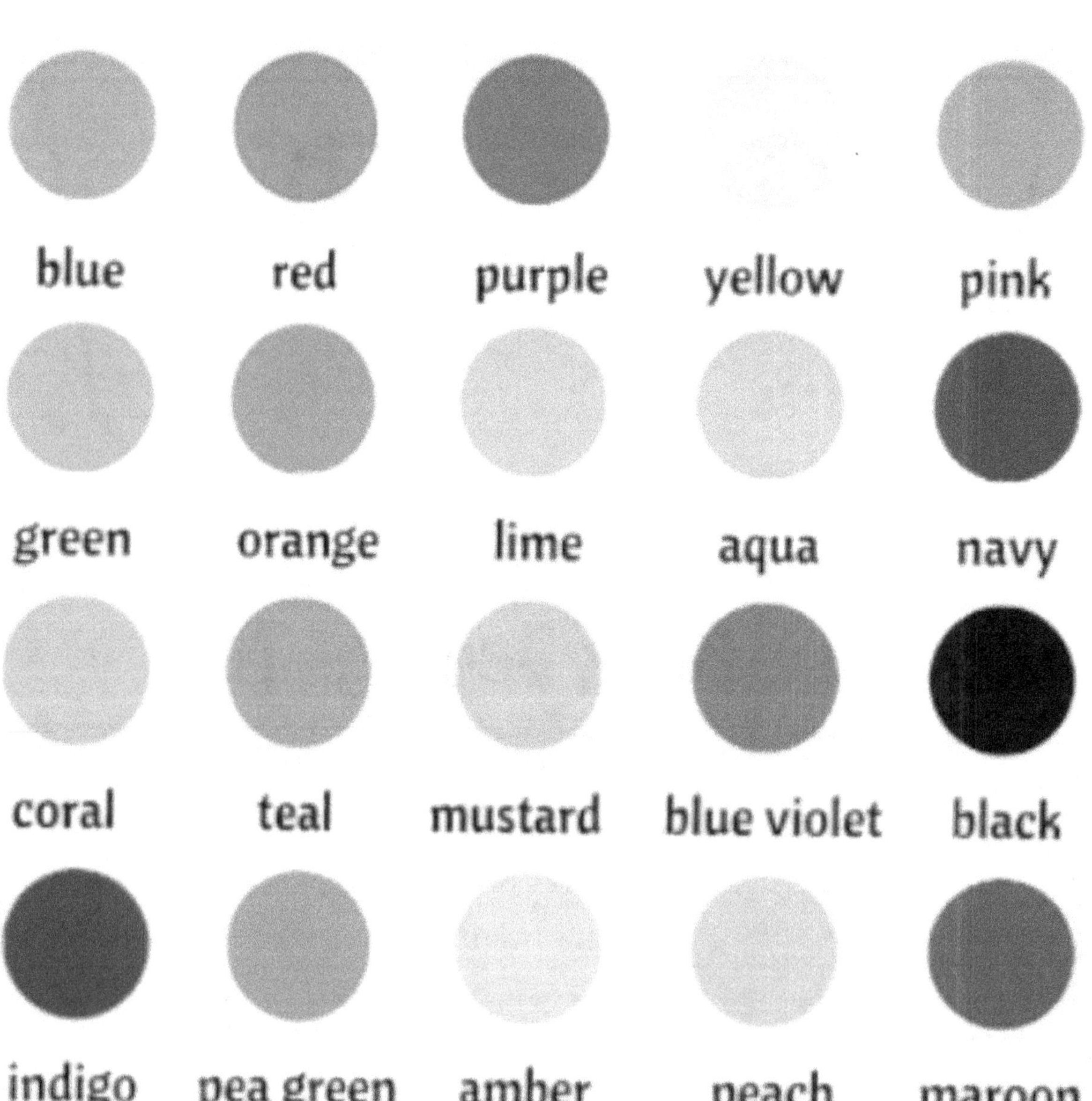

blue
red
purple
yellow
pink
green
orange
lime
aqua
navy
coral
teal
mustard
blue violet
black
indigo
pea green
amber
peach
maroon

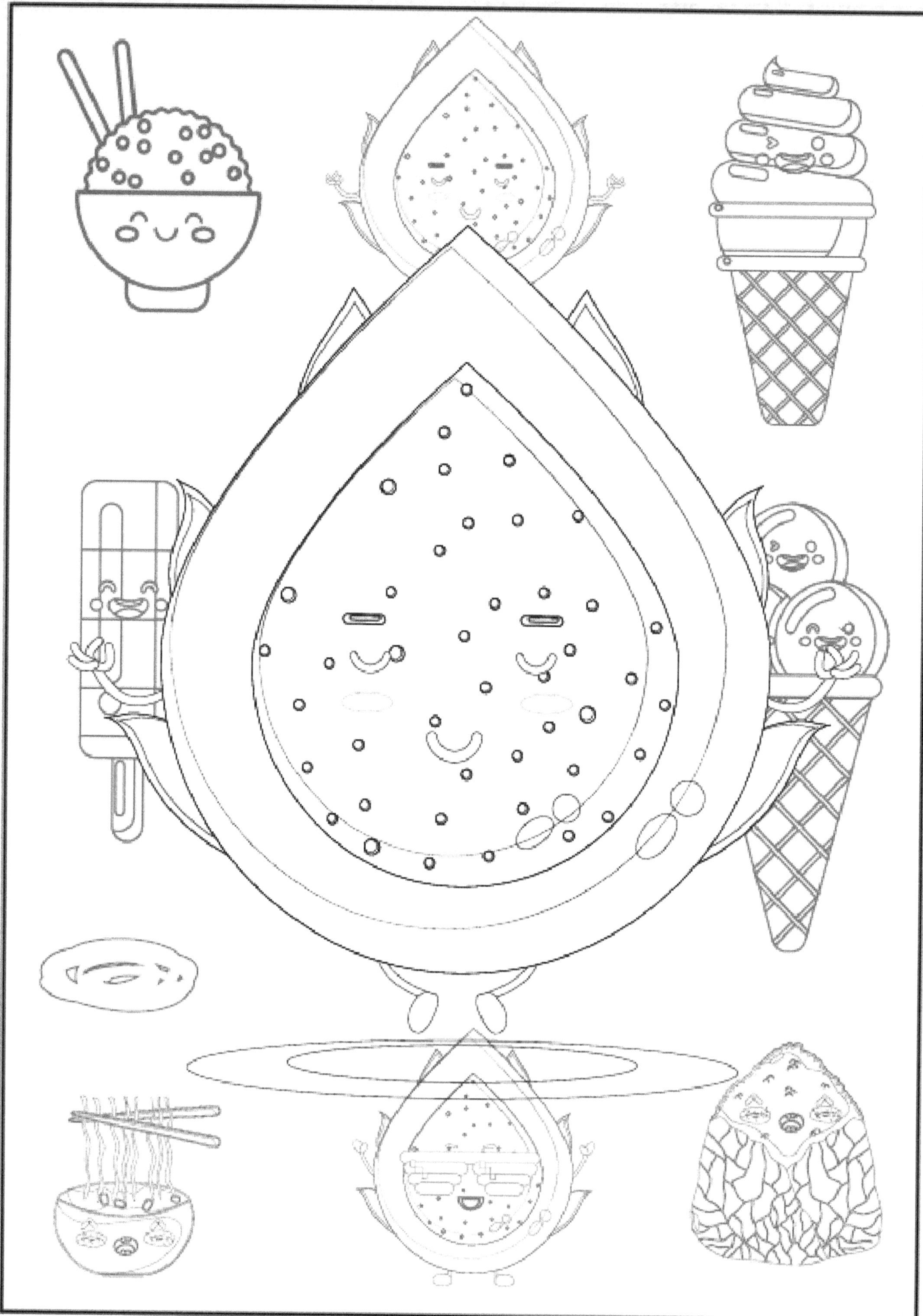

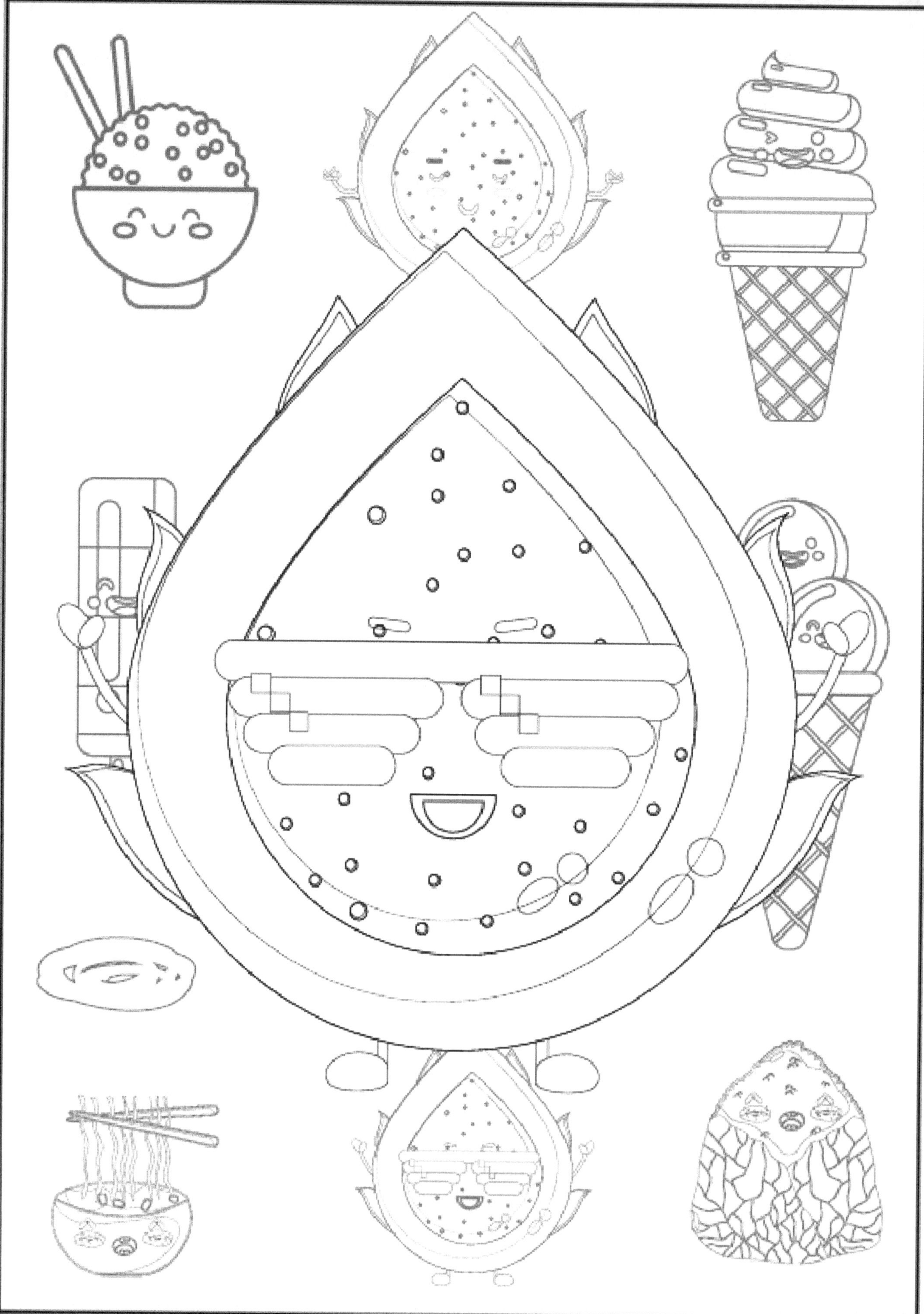

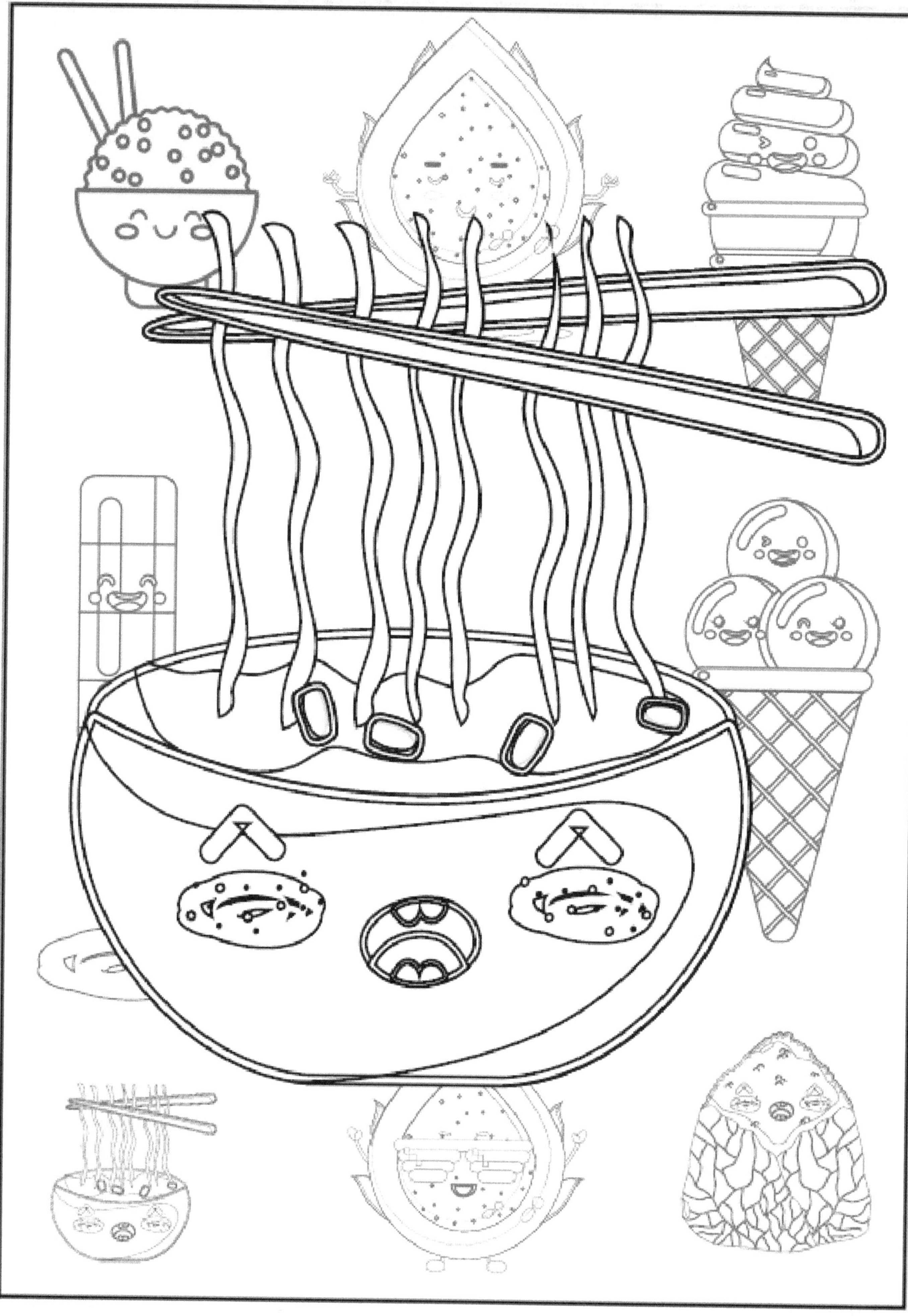

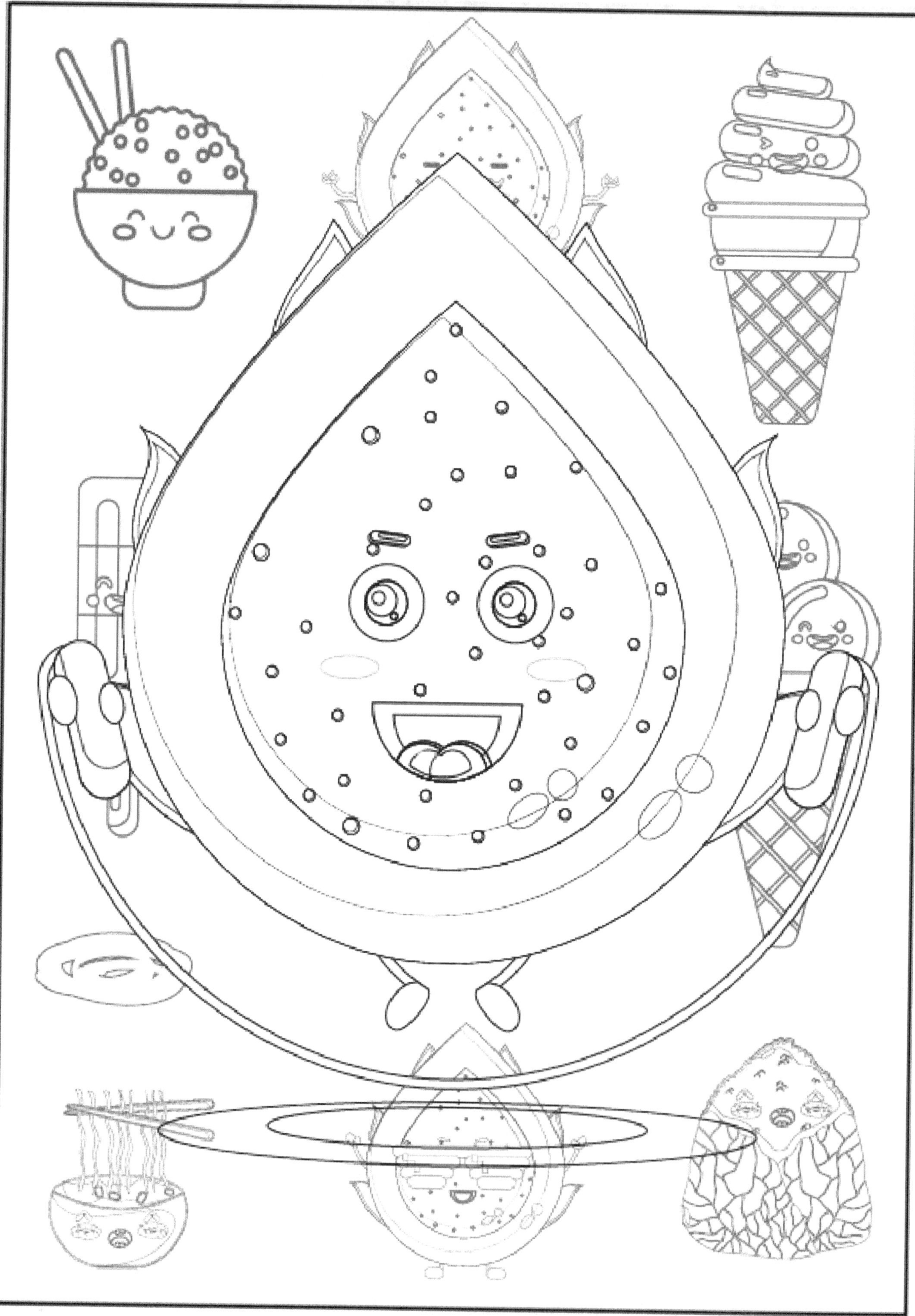

Fries

Fries

Fries

Fries

Fries

Fries

Fries

Fries

Fries

Fries

Fries

Fries

Fries

Fries

Fries

Fries